811
Smi   Smith, Tracy.
          Life On Mars

DATE DUE

BOOKS BY TRACY K. SMITH

Poetry
The Body's Question
Duende
Life on Mars

Memoir
Ordinary Light

LIFE ON MARS

POEMS

TRACY K. SMITH

GRAYWOLF PRESS

This publication is made possible by funding provided in part by a grant from
the Minnesota State Arts Board, through an appropriation by the Minnesota
State Legislature, a grant from the National Endowment for the Arts, and pri-
vate funders. Significant support has also been provided by Target; the McKnight
Foundation; and other generous contributions from foundations, corporations, and
individuals. To these organizations and individuals we offer our heartfelt thanks.

Published by Graywolf Press
250 Third Avenue North, Suite 600
Minneapolis, Minnesota 55401

www.graywolfpress.org

Published in the United States of America

ISBN 978-1-55597-584-5

12 14 16 18 17 15 13 11

Library of Congress Control Number: 2011920674

Cover design: Kyle G. Hunter

Cover photo: "Cone Nebula Close Up" © STScI

for Raf

CONTENTS

LIFE ON MARS

THE WEATHER IN SPACE

Is God being or pure force? The wind

Or what commands it? When our lives slow

And we can hold all that we love, it sprawls

In our laps like a gangly doll. When the storm

Kicks up and nothing is ours, we go chasing

After all we're certain to lose, so alive—

Faces radiant with panic.

ONE

SCI-FI

There will be no edges, but curves.
Clean lines pointing only forward.

History, with its hard spine & dog-eared
Corners, will be replaced with nuance,

Just like the dinosaurs gave way
To mounds and mounds of ice.

Women will still be women, but
The distinction will be empty. Sex,

Having outlived every threat, will gratify
Only the mind, which is where it will exist.

For kicks, we'll dance for ourselves
Before mirrors studded with golden bulbs.

The oldest among us will recognize that glow—
But the word *sun* will have been re-assigned

To a Standard Uranium-Neutralizing device
Found in households and nursing homes.

And yes, we'll live to be much older, thanks
To popular consensus. Weightless, unhinged,

Eons from even our own moon, we'll drift
In the haze of space, which will be, once

And for all, scrutable and safe.

MY GOD, IT'S FULL OF STARS

1.

We like to think of it as parallel to what we know,
Only bigger. One man against the authorities.
Or one man against a city of zombies. One man

Who is not, in fact, a man, sent to understand
The caravan of men now chasing him like red ants
Let loose down the pants of America. Man on the run.

Man with a ship to catch, a payload to drop,
This message going out to all of space. . . . Though
Maybe it's more like life below the sea: silent,

Buoyant, bizarrely benign. Relics
Of an outmoded design. Some like to imagine
A cosmic mother watching through a spray of stars,

Mouthing *yes, yes* as we toddle toward the light,
Biting her lip if we teeter at some ledge. Longing
To sweep us to her breast, she hopes for the best

While the father storms through adjacent rooms
Ranting with the force of Kingdom Come,
Not caring anymore what might snap us in its jaw.

Sometimes, what I see is a library in a rural community.
All the tall shelves in the big open room. And the pencils
In a cup at Circulation, gnawed on by the entire population.

The books have lived here all along, belonging
For weeks at a time to one or another in the brief sequence
Of family names, speaking (at night mostly) to a face,

A pair of eyes. The most remarkable lies.

2.

Charlton Heston is waiting to be let in. He asked once politely.
A second time with force from the diaphragm. The third time,
He did it like Moses: arms raised high, face an apocryphal white.

Shirt crisp, suit trim, he stoops a little coming in,
Then grows tall. He scans the room. He stands until I gesture,
Then he sits. Birds commence their evening chatter. Someone fires

Charcoals out below. He'll take a whiskey if I have it. Water if I don't.
I ask him to start from the beginning, but he goes only halfway back.
That was the future once, he says. *Before the world went upside down.*

Hero, survivor, God's right hand man, I know he sees the blank
Surface of the moon where I see a language built from brick and bone.
He sits straight in his seat, takes a long, slow high-thespian breath,

Then lets it go. *For all I know, I was the last true man on this earth.* And:
May I smoke? The voices outside soften. Planes jet past heading off or back.
Someone cries that she does not want to go to bed. Footsteps overhead.

A fountain in the neighbor's yard babbles to itself, and the night air
Lifts the sound indoors. *It was another time,* he says, picking up again.
We were pioneers. Will you fight to stay alive here, riding the earth

Toward God-knows-where? I think of Atlantis buried under ice, gone
One day from sight, the shore from which it rose now glacial and stark.
Our eyes adjust to the dark.

3.

Perhaps the great error is believing we're alone,

That the others have come and gone—a momentary blip—

When all along, space might be choc-full of traffic,

Bursting at the seams with energy we neither feel

Nor see, flush against us, living, dying, deciding,

Setting solid feet down on planets everywhere,

Bowing to the great stars that command, pitching stones

At whatever are their moons. They live wondering

If they are the only ones, knowing only the wish to know,

And the great black distance they—we—flicker in.

Maybe the dead know, their eyes widening at last,

Seeing the high beams of a million galaxies flick on

At twilight. Hearing the engines flare, the horns

Not letting up, the frenzy of being. I want it to be

One notch below bedlam, like a radio without a dial.

Wide open, so everything floods in at once.

And sealed tight, so nothing escapes. Not even time,

Which should curl in on itself and loop around like smoke.

So that I might be sitting now beside my father

As he raises a lit match to the bowl of his pipe

For the first time in the winter of 1959.

4.

In those last scenes of Kubrick's *2001*
When Dave is whisked into the center of space,
Which unfurls in an aurora of orgasmic light
Before opening wide, like a jungle orchid
For a love-struck bee, then goes liquid,
Paint-in-water, and then gauze wafting out and off,
Before, finally, the night tide, luminescent
And vague, swirls in, and on and on. . . .

In those last scenes, as he floats
Above Jupiter's vast canyons and seas,
Over the lava strewn plains and mountains
Packed in ice, that whole time, he doesn't blink.
In his little ship, blind to what he rides, whisked
Across the wide-screen of unparcelled time,
Who knows what blazes through his mind?
Is it still his life he moves through, or does
That end at the end of what he can name?

On set, it's shot after shot till Kubrick is happy,
Then the costumes go back on their racks
And the great gleaming set goes black.

5.

When my father worked on the Hubble Telescope, he said
They operated like surgeons: scrubbed and sheathed
In papery green, the room a clean cold, and bright white.

He'd read Larry Niven at home, and drink scotch on the rocks,
His eyes exhausted and pink. These were the Reagan years,
When we lived with our finger on The Button and struggled

To view our enemies as children. My father spent whole seasons
Bowing before the oracle-eye, hungry for what it would find.
His face lit-up whenever anyone asked, and his arms would rise

As if he were weightless, perfectly at ease in the never-ending
Night of space. On the ground, we tied postcards to balloons
For peace. Prince Charles married Lady Di. Rock Hudson died.

We learned new words for things. The decade changed.

The first few pictures came back blurred, and I felt ashamed
For all the cheerful engineers, my father and his tribe. The second time,
The optics jibed. We saw to the edge of all there is—

So brutal and alive it seemed to comprehend us back.

THE UNIVERSE IS A HOUSE PARTY

The universe is expanding. Look: postcards
And panties, bottles with lipstick on the rim,

Orphan socks and napkins dried into knots.
Quickly, wordlessly, all of it whisked into file

With radio waves from a generation ago
Drifting to the edge of what doesn't end,

Like the air inside a balloon. Is it bright?
Will our eyes crimp shut? Is it molten, atomic,

A conflagration of suns? It sounds like the kind of party
Your neighbors forget to invite you to: bass throbbing

Through walls, and everyone thudding around drunk
On the roof. We grind lenses to an impossible strength,

Point them toward the future, and dream of beings
We'll welcome with indefatigable hospitality:

How marvelous you've come! We won't flinch
At the pinprick mouths, the nubbin limbs. We'll rise,

Gracile, robust. *Mi casa es su casa.* Never more sincere.
Seeing us, they'll know exactly what we mean.

Of course, it's ours. If it's anyone's, it's ours.

THE MUSEUM OF OBSOLESCENCE

So much we once coveted. So much
That would have saved us, but lived,

Instead, its own quick span, returning
To uselessness with the mute acquiescence

Of shed skin. It watches us watch it:
Our faulty eyes, our telltale heat, hearts

Ticking through our shirts. We're here
To titter at the gimcracks, the naïve tools,

The replicas of replicas stacked like bricks.
There's green money, and oil in drums.

Pots of honey pilfered from a tomb. Books
Recounting the wars, maps of fizzled stars.

In the south wing, there's a small room
Where a living man sits on display. Ask,

And he'll describe the old beliefs. If you
Laugh, he'll lower his head to his hands

And sigh. When he dies, they'll replace him
With a video looping on *ad infinitum*.

Special installations come and go. "Love"
Was up for a season, followed by "Illness,"

Concepts difficult to grasp. The last thing you see
(After a mirror—someone's idea of a joke?)

Is an image of the old planet taken from space.
Outside, vendors hawk t-shirts, three for eight.

CATHEDRAL KITSCH

Does God love gold?
Does He shine back
At Himself from walls
Like these, leafed
In the earth's softest wealth?

Women light candles,
Pray into their fistful of beads.
Cameras spit human light
Into the vast holy dark,

And what glistens back
Is high up and cold. I feel
Man here. The same wish
That named the planets.

Man with his shoes and tools,
His insistence to prove we exist
Just like God, in the large
And the small, the great

And the frayed. In the chords
That rise from the tall brass pipes,
And the chorus of crushed cans
Someone drags over cobbles
In the secular street.

AT SOME POINT, THEY'LL WANT TO KNOW
WHAT IT WAS LIKE

There was something about how it felt. Not just the during—
That rough churn of bulk and breath, limb and tooth, the mass of us,
The quickness we made and rode—but mostly the before.

The waiting, knowing what would become. Pang. Pleasure then pain.
Then the underwater ride of after. Thrown-off like a coat over a bridge.
Somehow you'd just give away what you'd die without. You just gave.

The best was having nothing. No hope. No name in the throat.
And finding the breath in you, the body, to ask.

IT & CO.

We are a part of It. Not guests.

Is It us, or what contains us?

How can It be anything but an idea,

Something teetering on the spine

Of the number *i?* It is elegant

But coy. It avoids the blunt ends

Of our fingers as we point. We

Have gone looking for It everywhere:

In Bibles and bandwidth, blooming

Like a wound from the ocean floor.

Still, It resists the matter of false vs. real.

Unconvinced by our zeal, It is un-

Appeasable. It is like some novels:

Vast and unreadable.

THE LARGENESS WE CAN'T SEE

When our laughter skids across the floor
Like beads yanked from some girl's throat,
What waits where the laughter gathers?

And later, when our saw-toothed breaths
Lay us down on a bed of leaves, what feeds
With ceaseless focus on the leaves?

It's solid, yet permeable, like a mood.
Like God, it has no face. Like lust,
It flickers on without a prick of guilt.

We move in and out of rooms, leaving
Our dust, our voices pooled on sills.
We hurry from door to door in a downpour

Of days. Old trees inch up, their trunks thick
With new rings. All that we see grows
Into the ground. And all we live blind to

Leans its deathless heft to our ears
                                    and sings.

DON'T YOU WONDER, SOMETIMES?

1.

After dark, stars glisten like ice, and the distance they span
Hides something elemental. Not God, exactly. More like
Some thin-hipped glittering Bowie-being—a Starman
Or cosmic ace hovering, swaying, aching to make us see.
And what would we do, you and I, if we could know for sure

That someone was there squinting through the dust,
Saying nothing is lost, that everything lives on waiting only
To be wanted back badly enough? Would you go then,
Even for a few nights, into that other life where you
And that first she loved, blind to the future once, and happy?

Would I put on my coat and return to the kitchen where my
Mother and father sit waiting, dinner keeping warm on the stove?
Bowie will never die. Nothing will come for him in his sleep
Or charging through his veins. And he'll never grow old,
Just like the woman you lost, who will always be dark-haired

And flush-faced, running toward an electronic screen
That clocks the minutes, the miles left to go. Just like the life
In which I'm forever a child looking out my window at the night sky
Thinking one day I'll touch the world with bare hands
Even if it burns.

2.

He leaves no tracks. Slips past, quick as a cat. That's Bowie
For you: the Pope of Pop, coy as Christ. Like a play
Within a play, he's trademarked twice. The hours

Plink past like water from a window A/C. We sweat it out,
Teach ourselves to wait. Silently, lazily, collapse happens.
But not for Bowie. He cocks his head, grins that wicked grin.

Time never stops, but does it end? And how many lives
Before take-off, before we find ourselves
Beyond ourselves, all glam-glow, all twinkle and gold?

The future isn't what it used to be. Even Bowie thirsts
For something good and cold. Jets blink across the sky
Like migratory souls.

     3.

Bowie is among us. Right here
In New York City. In a baseball cap
And expensive jeans. Ducking into
A deli. Flashing all those teeth
At the doorman on his way back up.
Or he's hailing a taxi on Lafayette
As the sky clouds over at dusk.
He's in no rush. Doesn't feel
The way you'd think he feels.
Doesn't strut or gloat. Tells jokes.

I've lived here all these years
And never seen him. Like not knowing
A comet from a shooting star.
But I'll bet he burns bright,
Dragging a tail of white-hot matter
The way some of us track tissue
Back from the toilet stall. He's got
The whole world under his foot,
And we are small alongside,
Though there are occasions

When a man his size can meet
Your eyes for just a blip of time
And send a thought like SHINE
SHINE SHINE SHINE SHINE
Straight to your mind. Bowie,
I want to believe you. Want to feel
Your will like the wind before rain.
The kind everything simply obeys,
Swept up in that hypnotic dance
As if something with the power to do so
Had looked its way and said:

Go ahead.

SAVIOR MACHINE

I spent two years not looking
Into the mirror in his office.
Talking, instead, into my hands
Or a pillow in my lap. Glancing up
Occasionally to let out a laugh.
Gradually it felt like a date with a friend,
Which meant it was time to end.

Two years later, I saw him walking
Up Jay Street into the sun. No jacket,
His face a little chapped from wind.
He looked like an ordinary man carrying
Shirts home from the laundry, smiling
About something his daughter had said
Earlier that morning. Back before

You existed to me, you were a theory.
Now I know everything: the words you hate.
Where you itch at night. In our hallway,
There are five photos of your dead wife.
This is what we mean by sharing a life. Still,
From time to time, I think of him watching me
From over the top of his glasses, or eating candy

From a jar. I remember thanking him each time
The session was done. But mostly what I see
Is a human hand reaching down to lift
A pebble from my tongue.

THE SOUL

The voice is clean. Has heft. Like stones
Dropped in still water, or tossed
One after the other at a low wall.
Chipping away at what pushes back.
Not always making a dent, but keeping at it.
And the silence around it is a door
Punched through with light. A garment
That attests to breasts, the privacy
Between thighs. The body is what we lean toward,
Tensing as it darts, dancing away.
But it's the voice that enters us. Even
Saying nothing. Even saying nothing
Over and over absently to itself.

THE UNIVERSE: ORIGINAL MOTION PICTURE SOUNDTRACK

The first track still almost swings. High hat and snare, even
A few bars of sax the stratosphere will singe-out soon enough.

Synthesized strings. Then something like cellophane
Breaking in as if snagged to a shoe. Crinkle and drag. White noise,

Black noise. What must be voices bob up, then drop, like metal shavings
In molasses. So much for us. So much for the flags we bored

Into planets dry as chalk, for the tin cans we filled with fire
And rode like cowboys into all we tried to tame. Listen:

The dark we've only ever imagined now audible, thrumming,
Marbled with static like gristly meat. A chorus of engines churns.

Silence taunts: a dare. Everything that disappears
Disappears as if returning somewhere.

TWO

THE SPEED OF BELIEF

In memoriam, Floyd William Smith 1935–2008

I didn't want to wait on my knees
In a room made quiet by waiting.

A room where we'd listen for the rise
Of breath, the burble in his throat.

I didn't want the orchids or the trays
Of food meant to fortify that silence,

Or to pray for him to stay or to go then
Finally toward that ecstatic light.

I didn't want to believe
What we believe in those rooms:

That we are blessed, letting go,
Letting someone, anyone,

Drag open the drapes and heave us
Back into our blinding, bright lives.

When your own sweet father died
You woke before first light
And ate half a plate of eggs and grits,
And drank a glass of milk.

After you'd left, I sat in your place
And finished the toast bits with jam
And the cold eggs, the thick bacon
Flanged in fat, savoring the taste.

Then I slept, too young to know how narrow
And grave the road before you seemed—
All the houses zipped tight, the night's
Few clouds muddy as cold coffee.

You stayed gone a week, and who were we
Without your clean profile nicking away
At anything that made us afraid?
One neighbor sent a cake. We ate

The baked chickens, the honeyed hams.
We bowed our heads and prayed
You'd come back safe,
Knowing you would.

What does the storm set free? Spirits stripped of flesh on their slow walk.
The poor in cities learn: when there is no place to lie down, walk.

At night, the streets are minefields. Only sirens drown out the cries.
If you're being followed, hang on to yourself and run—no—walk.

I wandered through evenings of lit windows, laughter inside walls.
The sole steps amid streetlamps, errant stars. Nothing else below walked.

When we believed in the underworld, we buried fortunes for our dead.
Low country of dogs and servants, where ghosts in gold-stitched robes walk.

Old loves turn up in dreams, still livid at every slight. Show them out.
This bed is full. Our limbs tangle in sleep, but our shadows walk.

Perhaps one day it will be enough to live a few seasons and return to ash.
No children to carry our names. No grief. Life will be a brief, hollow walk.

My father won't lie still, though his legs are buried in trousers and socks.
But where does all he knew—and all he must now know—walk?

Probably he spun out of himself
And landed squarely in that there, his new
Body capable, lean, vibrating at the speed
Of belief. She was probably waiting
In the light everyone describes,
Gesturing for him to come. Surely they
Spent the whole first day together, walking
Past the city and out into the orchards
Where perfect figs and plums ripen
Without fear. They told us not to go
Tipping tables looking for them. Not even
To visit their bodies in the ground. They are
Sometimes maybe what calls out
To people stuck in some impossible hell.
The ones who later recall, "I heard a voice
Saying *Go* and finally, as if by magic, I was able
Simply to go."

What happens when the body goes slack?
When what anchors us just drifts off toward. . . .
What that is ours will remain intact?

When I was young, my father was lord
Of a small kingdom: a wife, a garden,
Kids for whom his word was Word.

It took years for my view to harden,
To shrink him to human size
And realize the door leading out was open.

I walked through, and my eyes
Swallowed everything, no matter
How it cut. To bleed was my prize:

I was free, nobody's daughter,
Perfecting an easy weightless laughter.

Of all the original tribes, the Javan has walked into the dappled green light.
Also the Bali, flicking his tail as the last clouds in the world dissolved at his back.
And the Caspian, with his famous winter mane, has lain down finally for good.
Or so we believe. And so I imagine you must be even more alone now,

The only heat of your kind for miles. A solitary country. At dawn, you listen
Past the birds rutting the trees, past even the fish at their mischief. You listen
The way a woman listens to the apparatus of her body. And it reaches you,
My own wish, like a scent, a rag on the wind. It'll do no good to coax you back

From that heaven of leaves, of cool earth and nothing to fear. How far.
How lush your bed. How heavy your prey. Day arrives. You gorge, sleep,
Wade the stream. Night kneels at your feet like a gypsy glistening with jewels.
You raise your head and the great mouth yawns. You swallow the light.

You stepped out of the body.
Unzipped it like a coat.
And will it drag you back
As flesh, voice, scent?

What heat burns without touch,
And what does it become?
What are they that move
Through these rooms without even

The encumbrance of shadows?
If you are one of them, I praise
The god of all gods, who is
Nothing and nowhere, a law,

Immutable proof. And if you are bound
By habit or will to be one of us
Again, I pray you are what waits
To break back into the world

Through me.

IT'S NOT

for Jean

That death was thinking of you or me
Or our family, or the woman
Our father would abandon when he died.
Death was thinking what it owed him:
His ride beyond the body, its garments,

Beyond the taxes that swarm each year,
The car and its fuel injection, the fruit trees
Heavy in his garden. Death led him past
The aisles of tools, the freezer lined with meat,
The television saying over and over *Seek*

And ye shall find. So why do we insist
He has vanished, that death ran off with our
Everything worth having? Why not that he was
Swimming only through this life—his slow,
Graceful crawl, shoulders rippling,

Legs slicing away at the waves, gliding
Further into what life itself denies?
He is only gone so far as we can tell. Though
When I try, I see the white cloud of his hair
In the distance like an eternity.

THREE

LIFE ON MARS

1.

Tina says what if dark matter is like the space between people
When what holds them together isn't exactly love, and I think
That sounds right—how strong the pull can be, as if something
That knows better won't let you drift apart so easily, and how
Small and heavy you feel, stuck there spinning in place.

Anita feels it now as a tug toward the phone, though she knows
The ear at the other end isn't there anymore. She'll beat her head
Against the rungs of her room till it splits, and the static that seeps out
Will lull her to sleep, where she'll dream of him walking just ahead
Beside a woman whose mouth spills *O* after *O* of operatic laughter.

But Tina isn't talking about men and women, what starts in our bodies
And then pushes out toward anywhere once the joy of it disappears.
She means families. How two sisters, say, can stop knowing one another,
Stop hearing the same language, scalding themselves on something
Every time they try to touch. What lives beside us passing for air?

2.

Last year, there was a father in the news who kept his daughter
Locked in a cell for decades. She lived right under his feet,
Cooking food, watching TV. The same pipes threading through his life
Led in and out of hers. Every year the footsteps downstairs multiplied.

Babies wailing through the night. Kids screaming to be let outside.
Every day, the man crept down into that room, bringing food,
Lying down with the daughter, who had no choice. Like a god
Moving through a world where every face looked furtively into his,

Then turned away. They cursed him to his back. He didn't hear.
They begged him for air, and all he saw were bodies on their knees.
How close that room. What heat. And his wife upstairs, hearing
Their clamor underfoot, thinking the house must just be

Settling into itself with age.

3.

Tina says dark matter is just a theory. Something
We know is there, but can't completely prove.

We move through it, bound, sensing it snatch up
What we mean to say and turn it over in its hands

Like glass sifted from the sea. It walks the shore,
Watching that refracted light dance back and forth

Before tossing whatever it was back to the surf.

4.

How else could we get things so wrong,
Like a story hacked to bits and told in reverse?—

5.

He grabbed my blouse at the neck.
All I thought was This is my very best
And he will ruin it. *Wind, dirt, his hands*
Hard on me. I heard the others
Jostling to watch as they waited
For their turns.

They were not glad to do it,
But they were eager.
They all wanted to, and fought
About who would go first.

We went to the cart
Where others sat waiting.
They laughed and it sounded
Like the black clouds that explode
Over the desert at night.

I knew which direction to go
From the stench of what still burned.
It was funny to see my house
Like that—as if the roof
Had been lifted up and carried off
By someone playing at dolls.

6.

Who understands the world, and when
Will he make it make sense? Or she?

Maybe there is a pair of them, and they sit
Watching the cream disperse into their coffee

Like the A-bomb. *This equals that,* one says,
Arranging a swarm of coordinates

On a giant grid. They exchange smiles.
It's so simple, they'll be done by lunchtime,

Will have the whole afternoon to spend naming
The spaces between spaces, which their eyes

Have been trained to distinguish. Nothing
Eludes them. And when the nothing that is

Something creeps toward them, wanting
To be felt, they feel it. Then they jot down

Equation after equation, smiling to one another,
Lips sealed tight.

7.

Some of the prisoners were strung like beef
From the ceilings of their cells. "Gus"
Was led around on a leash. I mean dragged.
Others were ridden like mules. The guards
Were under a tremendous amount of pleasure.
I mean pressure. Pretty disgusting. Not
What you'd expect from Americans.
Just kidding. I'm only talking about people
Having a good time, blowing off steam.

8.

The earth beneath us. The earth

Around and above. The earth

Pushing up against our houses,

Complicit with gravity. The earth

Ageless watching us rise and curl.

Our spades, our oxen, the jagged lines

We carve into dirt. The earth

Nicked and sliced into territory.

Hacked and hollowed. Stoppered tight.

Tripwire. The earth ticking with mines,

Patient, biding its time. The earth

Floating in darkness, suspended in spin.

The earth gunning it around the sun.

The earth we ride in disbelief.

The earth we plunder like thieves.

The earth caked to mud in the belly

Of a village with no food. Burying us.

The earth coming off on our shoes.

9.

Tina says we do it to one another, every day,
Knowing and not knowing. When it is love,
What happens feels like dumb luck. When it's not,
We're riddled with bullets, shot through like ducks.

Every day. To ourselves and one another. And what
If what it is, and what sends it, has nothing to do
With what we can't see? Nothing whatsoever
To do with a power other than muscle, will, sheer fright?

SOLSTICE

They're gassing geese outside of JFK.
Tehran will likely fill up soon with blood.
The *Times* is getting smaller day by day.

We've learned to back away from all we say
And, more or less, agree with what we should.
Whole flocks are being gassed near JFK.

So much of what we're asked is to obey—
A reflex we'd abandon if we could.
The *Times* reported 19 dead today.

They're going to make the opposition pay.
(If you're sympathetic, knock on wood.)
The geese were terrorizing JFK.

Remember how they taught you once to pray?
Eyes closed, on your knees, to any god?
Sometimes, small minds seem to take the day.

Election fraud. A migratory plague.
Less and less surprises us as odd.
We dislike what they did at JFK.
Our time is brief. We dwindle by the day.

NO-FLY ZONE

1.

She fears something but can't say what.
She goes in reverse, mopping up her own tracks.
When she sleeps, it's always the same foggy night.

The dead have stopped knocking. No answer.
Their big cars hover along her block, engines
Idling, woofers pumping that relentless bass

Into the bones of her house. All night they pass
Bottles cinched in bags back and forth
Through open windows.

I want to wake her. Drag her by the gown
Down into the street where her parents
Are alive again, laughing like stoned teenagers

At some idiot joke. Look, I want to say,
The worst thing you can imagine has already
Zipped up its coat and is heading back
Up the road to wherever it came from.

2.

She sends the air out of her lungs
Wanting to lie down
And fritter away like ash, thinking
Who would worry
If I marched into the sea
Till it rose around me like honey?

3.

Once upon a time, a woman told this to her daughter:

Save yourself. The girl didn't think to ask *for what?*

She looked into her mother's face and answered *Yes.*

Years later, alone in the room where she lives

The daughter listens to the life she's been saved from:

Evening patter. Summer laughter. Young bodies

Racing into the unmitigated happiness of danger.

4.

Out where the houses are low to the ground,
Dwarfed by overgrown trees and the ancient poles
Whose wires carry gossip from kitchen to kitchen,
The dogs run in packs, like children. The true children
Live indoors like sullen sages. *Pick up your bed and walk.*
You get used to doing nothing pretty quickly. Fish on Friday.
Biscuits-n-gravy. It's a sin to live behind curtains.
Pick up your bed and walk. Memory's stubborn—
I mean misery. You sit in silence waiting to be chosen.
Behaving. *Pick up your bed and walk.* You want it all
Over again. Past Perfect. But go back and they make you
Start from the beginning. Climb out, they put you right back in.
You lie there kicking like a baby, waiting for God himself
To lift you past the rungs of your crib. What
Would your life say if it could talk?

CHALLENGER

She gets herself so wound up. I think
She likes it. Like a wrung rag, or a wire
Wrapped round itself into a spring.

And the pressure, the brute strength
It takes to hold things that way, to keep them
From straightening out, is up to her

To maintain. She's like a kettle about to blow.
All that steam anxious to rise and go.
I get tired watching it happen, the eyes

Alive with their fury against the self,
The words swelling in the chest, and then
The voice racing into anyone's face.

She likes to hear it, her throat hoarse
With nonsense and the story that must
Get told again and again, no matter.

Blast off! she likes to think, though
What comes to mind at the moment
Is earthly. A local wind. Chill and small.

RANSOM

When the freighters inch past in the distance
The men load their small boats. They motor out,
Buzzing like mosquitoes, aimed at the iron
Side of the blind ship as it creeps closer.

They have guns. They know the sea like it
Is their mother, and she is not well. Her fish
Are gone. She heaves barrels leaking disease
Onto the shores. When she goes into a fit,

She throws a curse upon the land, dragging
Houses, people to their deaths. She glows
In a way she should not. She tastes of industry.
No one is fighting for her, and so they fight.

By night, they load their boats and motor out,
And by day, they aim their guns at the ships,
Climbing aboard. It is clear what they want.
The white men scramble. Some fight back.

When one is taken, the whole world sits up
To watch. When the pirates fall, the world
Smiles to itself, thanking goodness. They
Show the black faces and the dead black bodies

On TV. When the pirates win, after the great
White ships return to their own shores,
There is a party that lasts for days.

THEY MAY LOVE ALL THAT HE HAS CHOSEN
AND HATE ALL THAT HE HAS REJECTED

I.

I don't want to hear their voices.
To stand sucking my teeth while they
Rant. For once, I don't want to know
What they call truth, or what flags
Flicker from poles stuck to their roofs.

Let them wait. Lead them to the back porch
And let them lean there while the others eat.
If they thirst, give them a bucket and a tin cup.
If they're sick, tell them the doctor's away,
That he doesn't treat their kind. Warn them

What type of trouble tends to crop up
Around here after dark.

II.

Hate spreads itself out thin and skims the surface,
Nudged along by the tide. When the waves go all to chop,

It breaks up into little bits that scurry off. Some
Get snapped up by what swims, which gets snapped up

Itself. Hooked through the lip or the gills and dragged
Onto deck to bat around at the ankles of men who'll beat it,

Then scrape off the scales and fry it in oil. Afterward,
Some will sleep. And some will feel it bobbing there

On the inside. The night is different after that. Too small.
Something they swear could disappear altogether,

Could lift up and drift off, leaving only the sun,
Which doesn't have better sense than to cast its best light

On just anyone.

III.

Shawna Forde, Jason "Gunny" Bush and Albert Gaxiola,
Who killed Raul Flores and Brisenia Flores.

*It'll feel maybe like floating at first
And then a great current gets under you*

And James von Brunn, who killed Stephen Tyrone Johns.
And Scott Roeder, who killed George R. Tiller.

*And you ride—up to the ridge,
Over the side—feeling a gust of light*

And Stephen P. Morgan, who killed Johanna Justin-Jinich.
And Andrew Dunton, who killed Omar Edwards.

*Blasting through you
Like wind.*

IV: In Which the Dead Send Postcards to Their Assailants from America's Most Celebrated Landmarks

Dear Shawna,

How are you? Today we took a boat out to an island. It was cold even though the sun was hot on my skin. When we got off the boat, there was a statue of a big tall lady. My daddy and I rode in an elevator all the way up to the top of her head. My daddy says we're free now to do whatever we want. I told him I wanted to jump through the window and fly home to Arizona. I hope to become a dancer or a veterinarian.

Love,
Brisenia

Dear James,

I walked the whole Mall today, from the Capitol to the Lincoln Memorial. I thought I'd skip the Museum altogether, but my feet wanted to go there, so I let them. I stood outside the doors trying to see in, but it was so bright my own reflection was all that shone back at me. I can choose to feel or not to feel. I realized that today. Mostly it's just nice to move through the crowds like I used to: unnoticed. Only now they move through me too. Men, women, everyone, feeling untouched. But I've touched them. It's funny. I feel like myself. The breeze off the Potomac is calm.

Sincerely,
Stephen

Hello, Scott!

I thought of you today from a small grey pod inside the St. Louis Arch. We inched up, notch by notch, like some Cold War rendition of the womb. At the top, the doors yawned open and we pushed through the people waiting to go back down. The view's mostly of a stadium. On the other side, you see the old city in passive decline. You realize how small you are up there, but everyone still acts normal size. We were an assault on the sleek arch, silent and gleaming alongside the ageless Mississippi. But the guys on the ground keep selling tickets and sending more up. You can feel wind rocking the structure all the way at the top.

See you around,
George

S—

I'm happy. I'll probably be in Greece soon, or the mountains of Chile. I used to think my body was a container for love. There is so much more now without my body. A kind of ecstasy. Tonight, I'm at the bottom of the Grand Canyon. I don't know where I end. *The night is starry and the stars are blue and shiver in the distance.*

—J

Dear Andrew,

I'm still here. I don't think of you often, but when I do, I think you must look at people slowly, spinning through the versions of their lives before you speak. I think you must wonder what's under their coats, in their fists, what words sit warming in their throats. I think you feel humble, human. I hardly think of you, but when I do, it's usually that.

Yours,
Omar
Harlem, USA

V.

Or was it fear

Forde, "Gunny" and Gaxiola.

Like a bone caught in the throat

And James von Brunn.
And Scott Roeder.

Nicking at every breath, every word at the lips

And Stephen P. Morgan.

Like a joke that was on them

And Officer Andrew Dunton.

And no one to trust for help?

VI.

Line them up. Let us look them in the face.

They are not as altogether ugly as we'd like.
Unobserved, they go about their lives
With a familiar concentration. They pay

Their debts down bit by bit. They tithe.
They take the usual pride in their own devotion
To principle. And how radiant each is,

Touched by understanding, ready to stand
And go forth into that unmistakable light.
The good fight. One by one they rise,

Believing what to do, bowing each head
To what leads. And, empty of fear, buoyant
With the thrill of such might
                                    they go.

FOUR

THE UNIVERSE AS PRIMAL SCREAM

5pm on the nose. They open their mouths
And it rolls out: high, shrill and metallic.
First the boy, then his sister. Occasionally,
They both let loose at once, and I think
Of putting on my shoes to go up and see
Whether it is merely an experiment
Their parents have been conducting
Upon the good crystal, which must surely
Lie shattered to dust on the floor.

Maybe the mother is still proud
Of the four pink lungs she nursed
To such might. Perhaps, if they hit
The magic decibel, the whole building
Will lift-off, and we'll ride to glory
Like Elijah. If this is it—if this is what
Their cries are cocked toward—let the sky
Pass from blue, to red, to molten gold,
To black. Let the heaven we inherit approach.

Whether it is our dead in Old Testament robes,
Or a door opening onto the roiling infinity of space.
Whether it will bend down to greet us like a father,
Or swallow us like a furnace. I'm ready
To meet what refuses to let us keep anything
For long. What teases us with blessings,
Bends us with grief. Wizard, thief, the great
Wind rushing to knock our mirrors to the floor,
To sweep our short lives clean. How mean

Our racket seems beside it. My stereo on shuffle.
The neighbor chopping onions through a wall.
All of it just a hiccough against what may never
Come for us. And the kids upstairs still at it,
Screaming like the Dawn of Man, as if something
They have no name for has begun to insist
Upon being born.

EVERYTHING THAT EVER WAS

Like a wide wake, rippling
Infinitely into the distance, everything

That ever was still is, somewhere,
Floating near the surface, nursing
Its hunger for you and me

And the now we've named
And made a place of.

Like groundswell sometimes
It surges up, claiming a little piece
Of where we stand.

Like the wind the rains ride in on,
It sweeps across the leaves,

Pushing in past the windows
We didn't slam quickly enough.
Dark water it will take days to drain.

It surprised us last night in my sleep.
Brought food, a gift. Stood squarely

There between us, while your eyes
Danced toward mine, and my hands
Sat working a thread in my lap.

Up close, it was so thin. And when finally
You reached for me, it backed away,

Bereft, but not vanquished. Today,
Whatever it was seems slight, a trail
Of cloud rising up like smoke.

And the trees that watch as I write
Sway in the breeze, as if all that stirs

Under the soil is a little tickle of knowledge
The great blind roots will tease through
And push eventually past.

AUBADE

You wake with a start from some dream
Asking if I want to walk with you around the block.

You go through the things that need doing
Before Monday. Six emails. A presentation on Manet.

No, I don't want to put on clothes and shoes
And dark glasses and follow the dog and you

Down Smith Street. It's eight o'clock. The sun
Is toying with those thick clouds and the trees

Shake their heads in the wind. You exhale,

Wheel your feet to the floor, walk around to my side
And let your back end drop down onto the bed.

You resort to the weather. A high today of 78.
But that's hours away. And look at the dog

Still passed out cold, twitching in a dream.

When we stop talking, we hear the soft sounds
He makes in his sleep. Not quite barking. More like

Learning to speak. As if he's in the middle of a scene
Where he must stand before the great dog god

Trying to account for his life.

FIELD GUIDE

You were you, but now and then you'd change.
Sometimes your face was some or another his,
And when I stood facing it, your body flinched.
You wanted to be alone—left alone. You waded
Into streets dense with people: women wearing
Book bags, or wooden beads. Girls holding smoke
A moment behind red mouths then pushing it out,
Posing, not breathing it in. You smiled
Like a man who knows how to crack a safe.

When it got to the point where you were only ever
Him, I had to get out from under it, sit up
And set my feet on the floor. Haven't I lived this
Enough times over? It's morning, but the light's still dark.
There's rain in the garden, and a dove repeating
Where? Are? You? It takes a while, but a voice
Finally answers back. A long phrase. Over
And over. Urgently. Not tiring even after the dove
Seems to be appeased.

EGGS NORWEGIAN

Give a man a stick, and he'll hurl it at the sun
For his dog to race toward as it falls. He'll relish
The snap in those jagged teeth, the rough breath
Sawing in and out through the craggy mouth, the clink
Of tags approaching as the dog canters back. He'll stoop
To do it again and again, so your walk through grass
Lasts all morning, the dog tired now in the heat,
The stick now just a wet and gnarled nub that doesn't sail
So much as drop. And when the dog plops to the grass
Like a misbegotten turd, and even you want nothing
More than a plate of eggs at some sidewalk café, the man—
Who, too, by now has dropped even the idea of *fetch*—
Will push you against a tree and ease his leg between
Your legs as his industrious tongue whispers
Convincingly into your mouth.

THE GOOD LIFE

When some people talk about money
They speak as if it were a mysterious lover
Who went out to buy milk and never
Came back, and it makes me nostalgic
For the years I lived on coffee and bread,
Hungry all the time, walking to work on payday
Like a woman journeying for water
From a village without a well, then living
One or two nights like everyone else
On roast chicken and red wine.

WILLED IN AUTUMN

The room is red, like ourselves
On the inside. We enter
And my heart ticks out its tune
Of *soon, soon.* I kneel

On the bed and wait. The silence
Behind me is you, shallow breaths
That rustle nothing. This will last.
I grip the sheets, telling time

To get lost. I close my eyes
So the red is darker now, deep,
A willed distance that backs away
The faster we approach.

I dream a little plot of land and six
Kid goats. Every night it rains.
Every morning sun breaks through
And the earth is firm again under our feet.

I am writing this so it will stay true.
Go for a while into your life,
But meet me come dusk
At a bar where music sweeps out

From a jukebox choked with ragged bills.
We'll wander back barefoot at night,
Carrying our shoes to save them
From the rain. We'll laugh

To remember all the things
That slaughtered us a lifetime ago,
And at the silly goats, greedy for anything
Soft enough to crack between their teeth.

SONG

I think of your hands all those years ago
Learning to maneuver a pencil, or struggling
To fasten a coat. The hands you'd sit on in class,
The nails you chewed absently. The clumsy authority
With which they'd sail to the air when they knew
You knew the answer. I think of them lying empty
At night, of the fingers wrangling something
From your nose, or buried in the cave of your ear.
All the things they did cautiously, pointedly,
Obedient to the suddenest whim. Their shames.
How they failed. What they won't forget year after year.
Or now. Resting on the wheel or the edge of your knee.
I am trying to decide what they feel when they wake up
And discover my body is near. Before touch.
Pushing off the ledge of the easy quiet dancing between us.

ALTERNATE TAKE

for Levon Helm

I've been beating my head all day long on the same six lines,
Snapped off and whittled to nothing like the nub of a pencil
Chewed up and smoothed over, yellow paint flecking my teeth.

And this whole time a hot wind's been swatting at my door,
Spat from his mouth and landing smack against my ear.
All day pounding the devil out of six lines and coming up dry,

While he drives donuts through my mind's back woods with that
Dirt-road voice of his, kicking up gravel like a runaway Buick.
He asks *Should I come in with that back beat,* and whatever those

Six lines were bothered by skitters off like water in hot grease.
Come in, Levon, with your lips stretched tight and that pig-eyed grin,
Bass mallet socking it to the drum. Lay it down like you know

You know how, shoulders hiked nice and high, chin tipped back,
So the song has to climb its way out like a man from a mine.

SACRAMENT

The women all sing when the pain is too much.

But first there is a deep despairing silence.

I don't know what rocks in them, what wants

To knock them clear. Not just the child,

Who knows only to obey. This something

Takes them from chatter, to a silly dance,

Down to all fours begging to die. Then

It drags them up by the hair, or lays them out flat

And strikes them on the head. Then they see it,

So bright it should be death, commanding *now*.

And again, after a pause. *Now.* Nothing else

Is there between it and them. It burns the air,

Singes sound. Their voices sink deep into themselves,

Down through flesh into the body's own hell. Sometimes

It takes forever for that song only the animals know

To climb back up into air as if to burst the throat.

WHEN YOUR SMALL FORM TUMBLED INTO ME

I lay sprawled like a big-game rug across the bed:
Belly down, legs wishbone-wide. It was winter.
Workaday. Your father swung his feet to the floor.
The kids upstairs dragged something back and forth
On shrieking wheels. I was empty, blown-through
By whatever swells, swirling, and then breaks
Night after night upon that room. You must have watched
For what felt like forever, wanting to be
What we passed back and forth between us like fire.
Wanting weight, desiring desire, dying
To descend into flesh, fault, the brief ecstasy of being.
From what dream of world did you wriggle free?
What soared—and what grieved—when you aimed your will
At the *yes* of my body alive like that on the sheets?

US & CO.

We are here for what amounts to a few hours,

a day at most.

We feel around making sense of the terrain,

our own new limbs,

Bumping up against a herd of bodies

until one becomes home.

Moments sweep past. The grass bends

then learns again to stand.

NOTES

The title "My God, It's Full of Stars" is adapted from a quote from Arthur C. Clarke's novel, *2001: A Space Odyssey,* which reads "The thing's hollow— it goes on forever—and—oh *my God—it's full of stars!*" It is also the opening line to Peter Hyams's film, *2010.*

The title "Don't You Wonder, Sometimes?" is a quote from David Bowie's song "Sound and Vision," which was released on the 1977 album *Low.*

"Savior Machine" draws its title from David Bowie's "Saviour Machine," which appears on the 1970 album *The Man Who Sold the World.*

"The Speed of Belief": the Javan, Caspian, and Bali are species of tiger believed to have gone extinct.

The title "Life on Mars" is borrowed from David Bowie's song "Life on Mars?" released in 1971 on the album *Hunky Dory.* Passages within section 7 of the poem, which refers to prisoner abuse by US military personnel at the Abu Ghraib prison in Iraq, are taken from the following sources:

> "It was pretty disgusting, not what you'd expect from Americans" is a quote from Senator Norm Coleman (R) Minnesota, taken from "Weekly Review," *Harper's Magazine,* May 18, 2004.

> The May 4, 2004 *Rush Limbaugh Show,* titled "It's Not about Us; This Is War!":

> CALLER: It was like a college fraternity prank that stacked up naked men—

> LIMBAUGH: Exactly. Exactly my point! This is no different than what happens at the Skull and Bones initiation and we're going to ruin people's lives over it and we're going to hamper our military effort, and then we are going to really hammer them because they had a good time. You know, these people are being fired at every day. I'm talking about people having a good time, these people, you ever heard of emotional release? You ever heard of need to blow some steam off?

"They May Love All That He Has Chosen and Hate All That He Has Rejected" is based on the following *New York Times* reports from the spring of 2009:

On May 6, 2009, Stephen P. Morgan shot and killed Wesleyan undergraduate Johanna Justin-Jinich. A journal belonging to Morgan contained entries reading "I think it okay to kill Jews, and go on a killing spree at this school," and "Kill Johanna. She must die."

On May 28, 2009, off-duty NYPD Officer Omar Edwards was fatally shot by fellow Officer Andrew P. Dunton. Edwards, who was black, drew his weapon after encountering and racing after a man who was breaking into his car on East 123rd Street. Officer Dunton, one of three white officers in an unmarked police car patrolling the neighborhood, saw him racing down the street with his pistol in the air, and emerged from the car to shout, "Police! Drop the gun."

On May 30, 2009, Jason "Gunny" Bush, Shawna Forde, and Albert Gaxiola of the Minutemen American Defense group arrived at the home of Raul J. Flores dressed in uniforms resembling those of law-enforcement personnel. They opened fire, killing Flores and his nine-year-old daughter, Brisenia, and injuring his wife, Gina Gonzalez.

On May 31, 2009, late-term abortion practitioner Dr. George R. Tiller was shot and killed in the foyer of his church in Wichita, Kansas. Scott Roeder was taken into custody as a suspect in the shooting. Sixteen years earlier, Tiller was shot in both arms by abortion opponent Rachelle "Shelly" Shannon.

On June 10, 2009, James von Brunn, an eighty-eight-year-old white supremacist, entered the US Holocaust Memorial Museum and opened fire, killing thirty-nine-year-old security guard Stephen Tyrone Johns before being shot in the face by museum security.

The poem's title comes from "The Community Rule," one of the Dead Sea Scrolls discovered in Qumran during the mid-twentieth century.

The postcard from J (Johanna Justin-Jinich) to S (Stephen P. Morgan) ends with lines from Neruda's "Sonnet XX."

ACKNOWLEDGMENTS

Grateful acknowledgment is made to the editors of the following journals, who first published versions of these poems: the *Awl, Barrow Street, Bat City Review,* the *Believer,* the *Portable Boog Reader No. 5, Cimarron Review, Eleven Eleven,* the *New Yorker, Ploughshares, PMS: poemmemoirstory, Tin House, Zoland Poetry No. 4.*

"It & Co." was broadcast on BBC Radio 4's "Front Row" on October 15, 2010.

"Life on Mars" appears on rolexmentorprotege.com and brooklynpoetry.com.

The penultimate section of "The Speed of Belief" appears, in video format, on badilishapoetry.com as "Water, Shade."

"The Universe as Primal Scream" appears, in video format, on rolexmentorprotege.com.

I would like to thank Jericho Brown, Tina Chang, David Semanki, Mark Doty, Paul Lisicky, and Hans Magnus Enzensberger. Thanks also to the generous support of Princeton University and the Rolex Mentor & Protégé Arts Initiative, which contributed to the completion of this book.

TRACY K. SMITH was named Poet Laureate of the United States in 2017. She is the author of three poetry collections: *Life on Mars*, winner of the Pulitzer Prize; *Duende*, winner of the James Laughlin Award; and *The Body's Question*, winner of the Cave Canem Poetry Prize. She is also the author of a memoir, *Ordinary Light*, which was a finalist for the National Book Award. She has received awards from the Rona Jaffe and Mrs. Giles Whiting Foundations and has been a protégée in the Rolex Mentor & Protégé Arts Initiative. A professor of creative writing at Princeton University, she lives in Princeton with her family.

Book design and composition by BookMobile Design and Publishing Services, Minneapolis, Minnesota. Manufactured by Versa Press on acid-free 30 percent postconsumer watstepaper.